Happy 1st Anniversary

have

Mum, Alex, Sasha & Henry

X X X X

TORSTEN

&

Cheryl.

CW01066956

Classic
Pizza and Pasta
Recipes

W. Foulsham & Co. Ltd.
London • New York • Toronto • Cape Town • Sydney

Classic
Pizza and
Pasta
Recipes

Renato Rudatis

Introduction

Hardly any other cuisine has become so popular as the Italian. Even the best and most famous French chefs have had to study it to avoid being overshadowed by their accomplished Italian colleagues. Italian food is appealing because of its simplicity and the interplay of many different flavours, as well as its vast range of produce.

Every region, almost every city and every province in Italy boasts its own speciality, which is always superbly prepared. The gourmet in search of something novel has his tastebuds stimulated anew every day. In this book we want to introduce you to the best known and most popular of Italian dishes: pizza and pasta.

Even those who are not professional cooks will encounter no difficulties in following the recipes. The basic recipes are straightforward and simple, accompanied by clear illustrations to guide you through step by step. All recipes are for four people. It is easy to adjust the amounts required for one, two, three or more servings.

Eating means more to the gourmet than merely satisfying hunger: it means the social climax of his day. Therefore it almost goes without saying that Italians pursue their enjoyment of food with devout singlemindedness.

If you are planning an Italian meal, here are some suggestions about the sequence of dishes, and the customs at mealtimes.

Contents

To start, there is the aperitif which stimulates the diner as well as his taste buds. Then follows the *antipasta*, a selection of small delicacies: various salads, hams, smoked or cooked, sausages, particularly salami and mortadella, tiny pieces of fish, olives and the hearts of artichokes, sweet-sour vegetables; mild cheeses are also served with leavened bread, freshly baked white bread or rusks. The selection is enormous. For example, arrange green and black olives, slices of tomato, red pepper, lettuce and cheese on individual hors d'oeuvre plates, sprinkle with herbs and an olive oil dressing, and serve. It looks spectacular, is a joy to savour, and is quick and simple to prepare.

Primo platto, the first course, mostly consists of some kind of pasta. The Italians excel at this dish, be it in soup, in a sauce or filled like the famous lasagne and cannelloni. These farinaceous dishes are meant to satisfy hunger, so that the following course can be appreciated at leisure. That is to say, a meat, poultry or fish dish, and the dessert course.

The pasta dishes can be served as the main course, if you wish. Alternatively, choose a couple of pizzas from the selection of recipes on pages 20–39.

Anyone who has eaten a meal in Italy will be familiar with the obligatory items: a carafe of water, a basket filled with bread, the condiments including oil and vinegar, essential to the preparation of salads, and last but not least the carafes filled with light wines – all these are absolutely indispensable for the well-being of the Italians. Naturally, the *espresso* after the meal is a must. Sometimes the coffee is served with a dash of alcohol; for example, *espresso grotto* with *grappa* is an excellent aid to the digestion.

If you are considering having an Italian evening at home with friends, time should not be of the essence. It is leisurely conversation which makes for true enjoyment of Italian food.

Friends enhance a pleasant atmosphere and good food makes the occasion. Italian gourmets testify to this, but why don't you find out for yourself? We wish you much enjoyment and every success when following these mouthwatering pizza and pasta dishes.

Renato Rudatis

HERBS AND SPICES

In the following chapters we would like to give you a brief summary of the principal ingredients used in preparing pizza and pasta dishes. Herbs and spices are used as a matter of course in Italy, as they are in most countries, in order to enhance the flavour of a particular dish.

Food is not merely valued for its nourishing function, but by the judicious use of herbs and spices we are able to improve the appearance of a dish and at the same time to stimulate the tastebuds.

Every cook has a personal preference for herbs and spices, which makes each dish unique.

Here are some useful tips for your herb and spice store. One sprig of fresh herbs is the equivalent of 1 tsp dried herbs.

Fresh herbs should be added at the end of the cooking process in order to retain their flavour.

Dried herbs to be added immediately.

Dried herbs should be stored in airtight jars and preferably stored in a dark place, otherwise they lose their aroma.

It is possible to keep fresh herbs for a few days in the refrigerator, provided they have been sprinkled with water and placed in a well-sealed plastic bag.

The easiest way to keep fresh herbs is to freeze them. The herbs should be finely chopped and patted dry in a cloth, spread on a baking tray and frozen. When frozen, place in plastic bags and store in the freezer. Another method is to freeze them in cubes in ice-cube trays.

If you want to dry your own herbs, chop them, squeeze out any moisture and dry them in a very cool oven. Apart from parsley, chives and dill, all other types of herb can be treated in this way.

The following are herbs most commonly used by Italian cooks.

Basil

This is added, either dried or fresh, to pizzas, pasta dishes, tomato dishes, meat, fish and poultry, as well as to salads and vegetables. It is important not to add too much.

Tarragon

This herb is an important addition to fish dishes. Also very popular when added to pizzas, pasta dishes, sauces, salads, vegetarian dishes and mayonnaise. Tarragon vinegar is, of course, well known.

Garlic

As far as the Italians are concerned, garlic has the status of a vegetable since it is always used liberally in most dishes. It is important to remember that garlic is very strong. When adding it to delicately flavoured pasta dishes, it must be used with care so that it does not overwhelm. In order to distribute the flavour evenly, garlic should be finely chopped and crushed in salt.

Lovage

Normally added to soups, meat and poultry pasta dishes, this herb is also used to flavour casseroles.

Oregano

This is most commonly used in pizzas, and it also adds a special flavour to salads and sauces.

Rosemary

A popular herb that is suitable for flavouring lamb, duck, goose, beef and pork pasta dishes. It should be used sparingly, because it has a strong aroma.

Sage

Especially popular with Roman cooks. It is added to veal and poultry pasta dishes. In combination with other herbs, sage counteracts the fattiness of goose and pork.

Thyme

A herb that must be used sparingly, because its flavour is very dominant. It is added to pasta dishes, pizzas, salads and salad dressings, as well as to vegetables.

Fennel

This is popular with Italian cooks, particularly for adding to bread dough, offal, poultry and fish pasta dishes.

VEGETABLES

Italy, like no other country, is blessed with a multitude of vegetables. Throughout the year, markets display an abundance of different vegetables of which the Italians make full use when making pizza toppings and pasta dishes.

Culinary enthusiasts should avail themselves of the opportunity to visit an Italian fruit and vegetable market, and marvel at the colourful display as well as observe the expertise with which the Italian housewife examines and chooses the wares on offer.

Everyone should follow the example of the Italians who will not use anything but really fresh produce, because this will determine the flavour of the cooked dishes. (*See Vegetable Pizza on page 24, Mushroom Pizza on page 31, Peasant Spinach Pizza on page 39, Green Lasagne with Vegetables on page 56, Vegetable and Noodle Soup on page 62*)

Here are some of the most popular Italian vegetables.

Chard

Also known as Swiss chard, seakale beet, silver or white beet. It is prepared similarly to spinach, which it resembles in taste. The stalks or ribs can be treated like asparagus, or chopped and served as a vegetable accompaniment to a pasta dish.

Chicory

Most people are not very familiar with this term. However, radicchio and chicory are gradually getting better known outside Italy. The bitter taste of chicory makes an interesting addition to salads.

Artichoke

This is known as the queen of vegetables in Italy. They are harvested before flowering and consist of the tightly packed leaf-top and the fleshy green base. Boil in slightly salted water, to which lemon juice has been added, for approximately 40 to 45 minutes. After cooking, the

leaves should pull away. The heart makes a wonderful pizza topping in addition to a pasta sauce. However, before savouring the heart, the surrounding hairy choke has to be removed and discarded.

Fennel

Originally from Italy, where the plant is used extensively: raw, boiled, blanched, as a side dish. The most familiar types to us are the smaller Florentine and the slightly stronger-tasting Neapolitan fennel.

Aubergine

This is a cucumber-shaped vegetable, also known as eggplant. The dark, shiny, purple skin should be smooth and firm. Before preparing for cooking, the pulp should be sprinkled with salt, then well rinsed in order to dispel any unpleasant bitterness.

Broccoli

It is closely related to cauliflower, but has a more pronounced flavour. Spiced with garlic, it is served with meat and fish pasta dishes.

Courgettes

Italians like to use these on pizzas and raw in salads.

Tomatoes

Undoubtedly Italy's most popular vegetable, these are found in innumerable pizza toppings and pasta sauces. Mediterranean food without the 'golden apple' is inconceivable. The tomato as we know it today has been cultivated by Neapolitan growers. (*See Bread Pizza with Herbs and Tomatoes on page 36.*)

MEAT, HAM AND SAUSAGES

The Italians, like most people, enjoy their meat dishes.

Italian cooks make use of all the well-known types of meat in their pizza toppings and pasta dishes. The Italian inventive genius can always produce a surprise dish, be it beef, veal, pork, lamb, bacon, ham or sausage. (*See Pizza with Bolognese Sauce on page 33, Meat and Gorgonzola Calzone on page 39 and Tuscan-style Macaroni on page 47.*) Also included are the favourites, lasagne and cannelloni, using minced meat.

Another Italian speciality are the varieties of sausages and hams. Every region and most towns have their individual delicacies. Although eaten at any time, they are delicious in pasta sauces and pizza toppings. (*See Spaghetti with Tomatoes and Ham on page 45.*) It is now possible to buy the famous Milanese salami sausage or Parma ham outside Italy.

Here are some of the best known hams and sausages.

Mortadella

This is the most famous sausage, and comes from Bologna. It consists of pork and bacon, and is boiled.

There are, however, some varieties containing veal and/or beef. Different regions add different spices. Mortadella can now be purchased outside Italy.

Here are some of the names you will come across:

Mortadella Fiorucci
Mortadella Divina
Mortadella Suprema
Mortadella Oro
Mortadella Aurora
Mortadella Locartelli

Salami

Roughly translated, salami means 'salt meat'. There are so many different types of excellent salami that to mention them all would require a book on its own.

Salami is a sausage which, according to ancient recipes, contained strongly seasoned donkey, pork and bacon. The meat was then rolled tightly and stuffed into skins. The duration of the curing process took six months, during which time the outside of the sausage became covered by a dry, mould-like substance.

Nowadays, salami is made of beef, pork and bacon. Home-made salamis are usually more coarsely textured. (*See Pizza with Ham and Salami on page 25.*)

Usually available outside Italy, the best known are:

Salami Napoli
Salami Milano
Salami Cacciatore
Salami Romagnolo
Salami Calabrese
Salami Campagnolo
Salami Fellino
Salami Veneto

Parma Ham

The best known Italian ham is produced in the surrounds of Parma in the Emilia-Romagna region. Only superior meat is used. The salted ham is lightly smoked. Its distinctive flavour is due to being matured in the fabulous climate of the region. For 15 months, the hams mature in the special factories before being released for sale.

The following are some of the better known varieties:

Prosciutto San Daniele
Prosciutto Casalingo
Prosciutto Tirolese
Prosciutto Sultan senza Osso
Prosciutto Pascia senza Osso

FISH AND SHELLFISH

When looking at a map of Italy it becomes quite clear that, apart from the northern part, it is entirely surrounded by sea. This is probably the reason why the Italians are so expert at preparing tempting fish pasta dishes, such as Conchiglie with Mussels on page 44 or Farfalle with Seafood on page 46. Only a few regions have no access to the sea, but even there you find choice fish recipes. The distance from the sea plays no part in the quality of the dishes. There are plenty of freshwater fish in the interior of the country to provide a variety of menus.

There are many varieties of sea and freshwater fish as well as shellfish on offer. Thanks to technical progress it is now possible to serve these delicacies in our own homes. Many kinds of deep-frozen fish are now on sale here. Our native varieties lend themselves equally well to the preparation of Italian dishes.

Be they shrimps, prawns, crab, mussels or squid, no inventive cook is able to pass these delicacies displayed on the fish stalls without a thrill. (*See Tagliatelle with Mussel Sauce on page 49, Pink Spaghetti with Squid Sauce on page 50, Seafood Pizza on page 24, Four Seasons Pizza on page 32.*) Just consider tuna fish, pike, anchovies, sardines also.

Mussels

Sold alive in the shell, by the pint or weight. Wash mussels thoroughly, discarding any open or broken shells; they should close when tapped. When cooked, throw away any mussels that have not opened.

Prawns

These popular shellfish are usually sold boiled, with shells or peeled. Prawns in their shells make attractive garnishes.

Squid

Squid have long grey bodies with tentacles and a head. Use small squid, under 15 cm/ 6 inches in length, for best results. To prepare squid, pull away the head and tentacles from the body. Put the ink sac aside if needed for a pasta sauce. Discard the head and bony piece in the tail. Wash well.

Sardines

These are really young pilchards – small herring-like fish, only distinguished by some black spots. Immediately after being caught sardines are cleaned, then cooked and preserved in oil. Ideal as nutritious pizza toppings.

Anchovies

Anchovies are small herring-like fish. Commercially, they are boned and salted to preserve them, and canned. (*See Roman Pizza on page 29 and Anchovy Pizza on page 36.*)

(*See also Cannelloni with Prawns on page 57, Agnolotti with Pike on page 59 and Genoese Fish Soup on page 62.*)

PASTA

Italians eat pasta almost every day; it is part of life and has its place on every menu, whether as a main course, stuffed or in soup.

It is no longer the prerogative of the housewife to make her own pasta since it is now widely and excellently produced commercially. The only task that remains is to cook it. However, this has to be learnt. Italians prefer their pasta cooked 'al dente', that is slightly firm to the bite. It should never be sticky.

For four people you will need approximately 300 to 400g/10 to 14oz. Cook in 4 litres/7 pints boiling salted water. Add 1 tbsp olive oil to prevent the pasta sticking together. Cooking time depends on the size and shape of the pasta. Directions are found on the package. An approximate guide is to allow 3 to 8 minutes for small shapes, 10 to 15 minutes for the larger ones. It is advisable to stir the pasta occasionally with a wooden spoon to prevent sticking. When cooked, strain well and serve immediately in a heated dish or on individual plates.

Italy is not the only country with an abundance of different kinds of pasta for sale; it can now be bought almost everywhere else in the world.

Sauces are a vital addition, because without them a pasta meal would be a sorry sight. And Italian cooks excel at sauces. Fine sauces are countless, each one with its own individual flavour and exquisite enough to make the gourmet swoon.

A simple way of serving pasta is just to add some butter and sprinkle cheese over the dish. However, tomato sauce, fish, meat and poultry sauces – dark as well as light – are popular and are always lovingly prepared.

How to make home-made pasta will be explained in the chapter on page 40. Here we are only concerned with listing the main varieties which are commercially produced.

Long pasta

Spaghetti – long, thin, solid. The various sizes are known as *fidelini* or *capellini, vermicellini, vermicelli* and *spaghetti.*

Maccheroni (macaroni) – long, thin and hollow. The different sizes are known as *bucatini, maccheroni* and *zite.*

Linguine – long, thin ribbon noodles. According to size, they are called *linguine, bavette* and *trenette.*

Small shapes

Chifferi – horn shaped. They come in two sizes: *chifferi* and *chifferoni.*

Penne – short, hollow with squared-off edges. They come in the following varieties: *pennini, penne, mezze penne* and *penne lisce.*

Ditali – very small round hollow shapes. They come in the following sizes: *ditalini, ditali, mezze canneroni.*

Conchiglie – shell shaped.

Finto gnocco – short spiral shaped pasta.

Farfalle – pasta shaped like a butterfly.

Tortiglione – spiral shaped.

Cappelletti – oval shaped, like small hats.

Tagliatelle – popular ribbon noodles. They come in various widths. *Fettucine* is one kind.

Fusilli – spirals shaped into a nest.

Stuffed pasta and sliced strips

Cannelloni – stuffed, rolled-out dough tubes. May also be served hollow.

Lasagne – strips of dough used in various ways. Sold as *lasagne, mezze lasagne* and *lasagne verde* (green).

Ravioli – small squares stuffed with different kinds of filling.

Tortellini – small rings stuffed like ravioli.

Pasta for soups

Anellini – little round serrated rings.

Stelline – small star shapes.

Tempertine – the smallest variety, square in shape.

Quadrucci – a slightly larger version of the above.

Pernicette and **Tubetti** – small, hollow round shapes.

Semi d'orzo – shaped like grains of rice.

CHEESE

First-class cheese is produced throughout Italy. There is a long tradition of cheese making; based on this tradition, the quality of the cheeses has evolved. Each region has its own special cheese for individual dishes.

As far back as the Roman period the inclusion of cheese dishes was taken for granted, and many cheeses date from that time.

Today many farmers have their own recipes for cheese making, but these cheeses always remain within the family for home use. In the Pau Valley and wherever else

there is lush grazing, cheese is mainly produced from cow's milk. In central and southern Italy, the milk of goats and sheep is more widely used.

Commercially some excellent brands of cheese can be obtained, many of which are exported and can be purchased here. (*See Pizza with Four Cheeses on page 31*.)

Here are some well-known cheeses.

Parmigiano

Parmesan is a hard cheese. Normally used for grating, it is liberally sprinkled on pizzas and pasta, and used in sauces. There are two varieties, *Parmigiano reggiano* and *Grana Pardano*, but only the former, which originated in Parma, is entitled to the term *Parmigiano reggiano*. It takes two years for Parmesan cheese to mature. The older it is, the stronger its tangy sharp flavour becomes.

Pecorino

This is a hard cheese, made from sheep's milk. Much favoured by Italian cooks, like Parmesan it is used for grating.

Gorgonzola

Italy too has its blue-veined cheese, which is made with cow's milk and has a strong, well-seasoned flavour. A similar cheese is *Dolcelatte* made, however, with sweet milk.

Provolone

Familiar to travellers in Italy, this creamy cheese is usually oval in shape and should be eaten very fresh. The longer it is kept the sharper its flavour. A smoked version is also obtainable.

Stracchino

Stracchino is the generic term for a number of cheeses produced mainly in northern Italy. One of them is *Talleggio*. All are soft, slightly sour cheeses. *Gorgonzola* and *Crescenza* (eaten as a sweet) are closely related to the Stracchino cheeses.

Mozzarella

This cheese is mild and slightly sour tasting, and is most commonly used on pizzas. It used to be made with buffalo milk, but is now usually made with cow's milk. *Scarmorza* is similar to Mozzarella, but more difficult to obtain outside Italy. *Manteca* and *fior di latte* are comparable.

Bel Paese

A mild, very creamy cheese, Bel Paese is an essential part of the Italian cheese board. It is excellent for cooking and may be substituted for Mozzarella when making pizzas and pasta dishes.

Mascarpone

This is an unsalted raw cheese with a creamy consistency.

Fontina

This cheese is a favourite with gourmets the world over. Semi-hard and creamy, it originated in the Aosta valley, taking its name from the Fontin mountain.

Ricotta

Ricotta is a soft cheese, resembling cottage cheese. It is usually made with cow's milk, though the more popular version is made with ewe's milk.

WINE

It is difficult to produce a rough guide to Italian wines. Italy produces more than any other country. There are as many choice wines for sale as there are less good ones. Only since 1963 has Italy evolved a system for standardization. However, owing to the quantity of varieties produced, it still is not perfect. One can only suggest that the traveller seek out the first-class wines for himself, of which there is an abundance. Every day presents new surprises. We would like, nevertheless, to draw up a few guidelines.

According to government regulations wines are divided into those which are under constant supervision and those which are not controlled. A system was devised which was then subdivided.

Denominazione Semplice
The vines are cultivated only in one particular region and the grapes pressed according to traditional methods.

Denominazione d'Origine Controllata
The vineyards are strictly controlled as is the production of the wine. Bottles bear the label DOC.

Denominazione d'Origine Controllata e Garantita
Only top-class wines are entitled to display this special seal, which is only issued after official inspection. The bottles are labelled DOCG.

A short glossary may serve to interpret different terms in use.

Abboccato – delicious, sweet

Amabile – delicious, not as sweet as *abboccato*

Amaro – bitter

Asciutto – very dry

Bianco – white

Cantina sociale – wine producers' cooperative

Chiaretto – pale red wine or rosé

Classico – classic

Dolce – sweet

Frizzante – effervescent

Gradazione alcolica – alcohol content

Liquoroso – liqueur

Nero – black, deep red

Pastosa – semi-dry

Produttore – producer, manufacturer

Riserva – fine wine produced according to DOC regulations

Rosato – rosé

Rosso – red

Secco – dry

Semisecco – semi dry

Stravecchio – matured according to DOC rules

Spumante – sparkling

Vino da pasto – table wine

Vino da tavola – table wine, not controlled

We now propose to explore some of the wine-growing regions. As mentioned before, it is impossible to list all the top-quality wines. Let us start with Piedmont, a region incomparably rich in its produce: a true paradise for both the gourmet and the connoisseur of fine wines. The list of white wines produced in this region is short. The Cortese grape, however, deserves mention: it is the source of Asti Spumante, a sweet, sparkling wine widely known beyond the frontiers of Italy and exported extensively. The principal produce in this region, however, is red wine, the best-known grape being the Nebbiolo. It goes into the making of such famous wines as Barolo and Barbaresco. Another Piedmontese wine is made from the Barbera grapes and is also very popular. Other varieties, equally good, are the wines made from the Dolcetto grape, for example Dolcetto d'Asti or Dolcetto d'Alba. The Freisa grape is cultivated in the area around Turin, Asti and Cuneo, and produces excellent wine. The above mentioned are but a few which are grown and there are many more that deserve mention.

We will now move on to the Veneto where there is a different wine eldorado. Verona close to Lake Garda and its fabulous vineyards is referred to sometimes as the capital wine city. Such well-known wines as Bardolino, Soave and Valpolicella are produced there. The Lambrusco from the Emilia-Romana district must not go without a mention.

Tuscany is another first-class wine-growing region. It is the home of Italy's best-known wine, Chianti. This wine is made from the Sangiovese grape and sometimes crossed with the Trebbiano and Cansiolo white grape, as well as some other varieties.

Equally well-known Tuscan wines are Brunello, and Vino Nobile de Montepulciano.

Orvieto, another great wine, comes from Umbria; it is pale golden in colour and full bodied.

Latium also produces first-class wines such as the famous Frascati. There are many varieties of this wine, golden in colour, full bodied with a dominant flavour.

Pizza

Nowadays, pizza is on everybody's lips, yet it was already well known in Roman times, as witnessed by the Pompeiian murals.

If one researches even further back into history one comes across a term used about 2,000 years ago in the Middle East. The word 'pitta' meant bread. The recipe travelled from the Middle East to Italy were innovative cooks created the versatile pizza. Whether served as a supper, snack or main meal, the pizza provides mouthwatering family fare and low-cost entertaining.

NOTES

Two different kinds of yeast dough are used in the making of pizza paste: the crumbly yeast dough and the medium-hard yeast dough. Strong plain flour, the main ingredient, should be tacky.

Both fresh and dried yeast act as raising agents. The rising of the dough can be accelerated at 30°C/85°F. Above 60°C/140°F the rising is complete. The finished pastry base lends itself well for deep freezing.

Crumbly Yeast Dough

Serves 4:

400g/14oz plain flour

1 tbsp sugar

1½ tsp salt

100g/4oz butter or margarine

25g/1oz yeast

250ml/8 fl oz warm milk

2 tbsp olive oil

1. Sift the flour on to a working top. Make a well in the centre and add the sugar and salt.

2. Scatter the butter in small pieces over the flour and rub in with the fingertips.

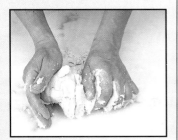

3. Dissolve the yeast in the warm milk and add the oil. Mix into the dough.

4. Knead into a smooth paste and shape into a ball. Make incisions with a knife and sprinkle with flour. Set aside.

Medium-Hard Yeast Dough

Serves 4:

400g/14oz plain flour

25g/1oz yeast

1 tbsp sugar

250ml/8 fl oz warm water

1½ tsp salt

2 tbsp oil

1. Sift the flour into a bowl and make a well in the centre. Crumble in the yeast, then add the sugar.

2. Add the water, cover with a cloth and leave to rise in a warm place for 30 minutes.

3. Add the salt and oil and beat into a smooth paste with a wooden spoon.

4. Knead into a ball. With a knife, make criss-cross incisions. Sprinkle with flour and leave until required.

Pizza Napoletana

(Neapolitan Pizza)

Serves 4:

25g/1oz butter or margarine

2 onions

250g/8oz ham

1 tbsp oregano

salt

freshly ground pepper

8 large tomatoes

1 small can anchovy fillets

20 black olives

1 recipe medium-hard yeast dough (page 22)

4 tbsp tomato purée

200g/7oz Mozzarella cheese

chopped parsley, to garnish

1. Chop the onions. Heat the butter in a pan and fry the onions until softened.
2. Cut the ham into cubes and cook gently for 2 to 3 minutes.
3. Season with the oregano, salt and pepper. Remove from heat and allow to cool.
4. Meanwhile skin and slice the tomatoes. Rinse the anchovy fillets and set aside the olives.

5. Cut the yeast dough into quarters. Roll out on a floured work surface and use to line 4 greased pizza or flan tins.

6. Spread the tomato purée over the dough. Cover with the ham and onions, the tomato slices, anchovy fillets and olives.

7. Slice the Mozzarella cheese and cover the pizza. Bake in a preheated oven at 200°C, 400°F, Gas Mark 6 for 20 minutes.
8. Serve sprinkled with parsley.

Pizza Frutti di Mare

(Seafood Pizza)

Serves 4:

8 medium tomatoes

100g/4oz shrimps

100g/4oz mussels, shelled

100g/4oz prepared squid

100g/4oz ham

200g/7oz Provolone cheese, grated

½ sprig basil, chopped

½ sprig oregano, chopped

475 ml/16 fl oz white sauce

1 recipe crumbly yeast dough
(page 22)

4 tbsp breadcrumbs

1. Skin and slice the tomatoes.
2. Set aside the shrimps, mussels and squid.
3. Cut the ham into thin strips.
4. Add the cheese and the herbs to the sauce and mix together.
5. Cut the yeast dough into quarters. Roll out on a floured work surface and use to line 4 greased pizza or flan tins.
6. Sprinkle the dough with the breadcrumbs, cover with the tomatoes and distribute remaining ingredients evenly.
7. Cover with the cheese sauce. Bake in a preheated oven at 200°C, 400°F, Gas Mark 6 for about 20 minutes.

Pizza alla Verdure

(Vegetable Pizza)

Serves 4:

100g/4oz streaky bacon

25g/1oz butter or margarine

2 onions

1 courgette

1 red pepper

1 green pepper

1 bunch spring onions

100g/4oz button mushrooms,
a few chillies

1 recipe medium-hard yeast dough
(page 22)

4 tbsp tomato purée

2 tbsp oregano

salt and freshly ground pepper

1 tsp garlic salt

200g/7oz Bel Paese cheese, grated

chopped chives, to garnish

1. Cut the bacon into small cubes. Heat the butter in a pan and cook the bacon.
2. Finely chop the onions, add to the pan and gently fry.
3. Slice the courgette. Cut the peppers into strips.
4. Trim and halve the spring onions lengthwise. Slice the button mushrooms. Rinse the chillies.
5. Cut the yeast dough into quarters. Roll out on a floured work surface and use to line 4 greased pizza or flan tins.
6. Spread the tomato purée over the dough. Distribute the remaining ingredients evenly and season with oregano, salt, pepper and garlic salt.
7. Sprinkle with the cheese. Bake in a preheated oven at 200°C, 400°F, Gas Mark 6 for about 20 minutes.
8. Serve sprinkled with the chives.

Pizza alla Macellaio

(Pizza with Ham and Salami)

Serves 4:

1 medium can peeled tomatoes

2 garlic cloves

1 tsp salt

2 tbsp olive oil

½ sprig oregano, chopped

1 recipe medium-hard yeast dough (page 22)

150g/5oz ham

100g/4oz salami

12 artichoke hearts

20 black olives

freshly ground pepper

200g/7oz Provolone cheese, grated

chopped oregano, to garnish

1. Drain the tomatoes well. Crush the garlic cloves in the salt.
2. Heat the oil in a pan and lightly fry the garlic.
3. Add the tomatoes and cook until the moisture has evaporated.
4. Remove from the heat and allow to cool. Add the oregano to the tomato mixture.
5. Cut the yeast dough into quarters. Roll out on a floured work surface and use to line 4 greased pizza or flan tins.
6. Spread the tomato mixture over the dough.
7. Cut the ham and salami into strips. Place on dough with the olives and artichoke hearts.
8. Season with salt and pepper and sprinkle with the cheese.
9. Bake in a preheated oven 200°C, 400°F, Gas Mark 6 for about 20 minutes. Serve sprinkled with the oregano.

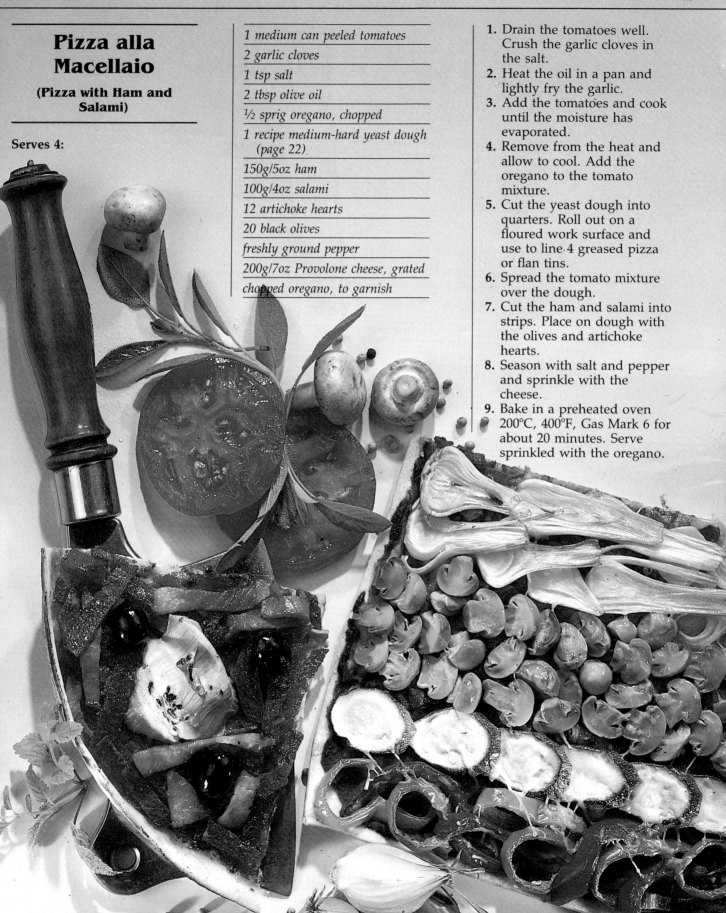

Calzone alla Cantiniera

(Vintner's Calzone)

Serves 4:

100g/4oz streaky bacon

25g/1oz butter or margarine

1 onion

1 bunch spring onions

100g/4oz button mushrooms

4 tomatoes

200g/7oz black grapes

12 stuffed olives

4 frankfurters

1 recipe crumbly yeast dough (page 22)

1 sprig oregano, chopped

salt

freshly ground pepper

200g/7oz Mozzarella cheese

1. Cut the bacon into small cubes. Heat the butter in a pan and fry the bacon.
2. Finely chop the onions and slice the spring onions. Add to the pan and cook until softened.
3. Wipe the button mushrooms and slice.

4. Skin the tomatoes, remove the seeds and cut into cubes.
5. Stone the grapes and set the olives aside.
6. Cut the frankfurters into cubes or thin slices. Mix all the ingredients carefully in a bowl.
7. Cut the dough into 4 large pieces. Roll out on a floured work surface.
8. Cover half of each piece of dough with the mixture. Sprinkle with the chopped oregano and season with salt and pepper.
9. Slice the cheese and place on top of the mixture. Fold over the other half of the dough into a pasty shape. Press the edges together.
10. Place on a greased baking tray. Bake in a preheated oven at 200°C, 400°F, Gas Mark 6 for about 20 minutes.

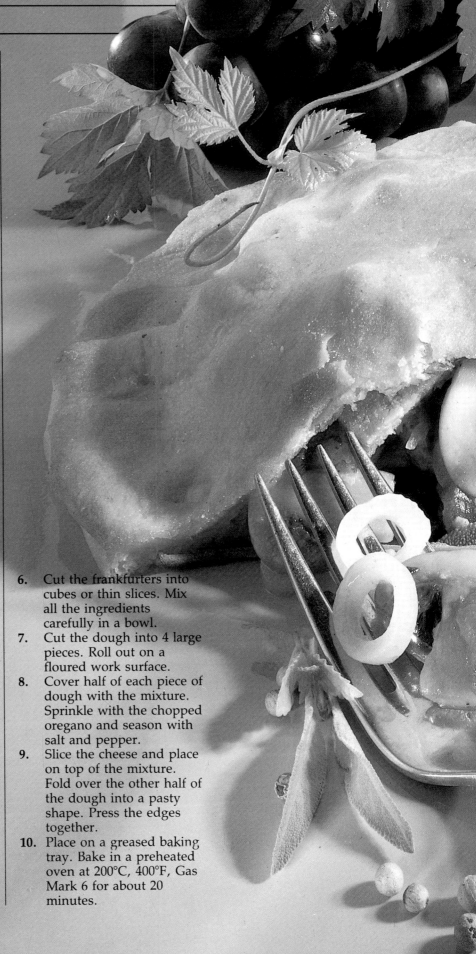

2. Finely chop the onion, add to the pan and cook until softened.
3. Drain the spinach and add to the bacon and onions. Season with salt and pepper, and a pinch of cayenne pepper and nutmeg.
4. Skin the tomatoes, remove the seeds and cut into cubes. Add to the spinach mixture. Remove the pan from the heat and allow to cool.
5. Meantime, cut the dough into 4 even portions. Roll out on a floured work surface.
6. Spread half of each portion with the mixture and sprinkle with the cheese and chopped chives.

7. Fold over the other half of the portion into a pasty shape. Press the edges together firmly.

8. Place on a greased baking tray or tin. Bake in a preheated oven at 200°C, 400°F, Gas Mark 6 for about 20 minutes.

Calzone d'Estate

(Summer Calzone)

Serves 4:

100g/4oz streaky bacon

25g/1oz butter or margarine

1 onion

200g/7oz frozen spinach, thawed

salt

freshly ground pepper

pinch cayenne pepper

pinch grated nutmeg

4 tomatoes

1 recipe crumbly yeast dough (page 22)

200g/7 oz Pecorino cheese, grated

½ bunch chives, chopped

1. Cut the bacon into small cubes. Heat the butter in a pan and lightly fry the bacon.

Shortcrust Pastry

Serves 4:

400g/14oz flour

1 tsp baking powder

1 tsp sugar

1 tsp salt

150g/5oz butter or margarine

2 eggs

NOTES

Shortcrust pastry is rich in fat, which gives it its character. Only best quality fats should be used. Egg yolks bind and facilitate the kneading of the dough; the whites serve to make it crisp. Shortcrust pastry is easy to keep. Wrapped in aluminium foil, it can be kept in the refrigerator for several days.

1. Sift the flour on to a work surface.

2. Mix in the sugar and salt.

3. Rub the butter into the flour with the fingertips. Add the eggs.

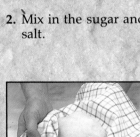

4. Knead from the outside inwards for a firm dough.

5. Wrap in a damp cloth and leave for 1 hour in the refrigerator.

6. Roll out the dough on a floured work surface. Grease a flan tin and fill with the dough.

Pizza alla Romana

(Roman Pizza)

Serves 4:

2 onions

25g/1oz butter or margarine

2 garlic cloves

1 tsp salt

1 small can peeled tomatoes

salt

freshly ground pepper

pinch mixed spices

8 tomatoes

250g/8oz can tuna fish in oil

1 can anchovy fillets

1 small can button mushrooms

20 black olives

2 eggs, hard boiled

8 green peppers

1 recipe shortcrust pastry
(page 28)

200g/7oz Crescenza cheese, grated

chopped parsley, to garnish

1. Finely chop the onions. Heat the butter in a pan and gently fry the onions until softened.
2. Crush the garlic cloves in salt (above). Add to the pan.
3. Add the peeled tomatoes; season with salt, pepper and mixed spices. Simmer until the mixture becomes a thick sauce.
4. Skin and slice the tomatoes.
5. Drain the tuna fish, anchovy fillets and button mushrooms.
6. Set aside the olives; slice the eggs and wash the peppers.
7. Cut the dough into quarters. Roll out and use to line 4 flan tins. Distribute ingredients evenly on top.
8. Sprinkle with the cheese. Bake in a preheated oven at 200°C, 400°F, Gas Mark 6 for 15 to 20 minutes.
9. Serve sprinkled with chopped parsley.

Pizza ai Quattro Formaggi

(Pizza with Four Cheeses)

Serves 4:

1 recipe shortcrust pastry
  (page 28)

4 tbsp tomato purée

8 tomatoes

250g/8oz ham

1 small can button mushroom

20 green olives

salt

freshly ground pepper

sprig oregano, chopped

50g/2oz Gorgonzola cheese, grated

50g/2oz Bel Paese cheese, grated

50g/2oz Mozzarella cheese, grated

50g/2oz Pecorino cheese, grated

1. Cut the dough into quarters. Roll out and use to line 4 greased flan or pizza tins.
2. Cover each base with 1 tbsp tomato purée.
3. Skin the tomatoes, slice and place on the bases.

4. Cut the ham into strips and slice the mushrooms. Place evenly on the pizza.
5. Stone the olives and add to the pizzas.
6. Sprinkle with salt, pepper and chopped oregano.

7. Use a quarter of each grated cheese to cover a quarter of each pizza.
8. Bake in a preheated oven at 200°C, 400°F, Gas Mark 6 for 15 to 20 minutes. Serve immediately.

Pizza ai Funghi

(Mushroom Pizza)

Serves 4:

100g/4oz streaky bacon

25g/1oz butter or margarine

1 garlic clove

1 tsp salt

1 onion

150g/5oz chanterelle mushrooms

150g/5oz yellow boletus
  mushrooms

4 tomatoes

100g/4oz ham

sprig parsley, chopped

½ bunch chives, chopped

salt

freshly ground pepper

pinch grated nutmeg

1 recipe shortcrust pastry
  (page 28)

200g/7oz Mozzarella cheese

1. Cut the bacon into cubes. Heat the butter in a pan and fry the bacon.
2. Crush the garlic in salt and fry lightly.
3. Finely chop the onions and allow to soften in the pan.
4. Clean the mushrooms; skin and seed the tomatoes, and cut the ham into strips. Add to the bacon and onions in the pan.
5. Mix together the chopped herbs and sprinkle over the mixture. Add salt, pepper and nutmeg to taste.
6. Cut the dough into four. Roll out and use to line 4 greased pizza or flan tins.
7. Distribute the mushroom mixture evenly over the dough. Slice the Mozzarella cheese and cover the pizzas.
8. Bake in a preheated oven at 200°C, 400°F, Gas Mark 6 for 15 to 20 minutes. Serve immediately.

Pizza Quattro Stagioni

(Four Seasons Pizza)

Serves 4:

1 recipe shortcrust pastry (page 28)

4 tbsp tomato purée

1 tbsp oregano

100g/4oz Parmesan cheese, grated

8 tomatoes

100g/4oz shrimps

100g/4oz mussels, shelled

100g/4oz ham

100g/4oz salami

1 small can button mushrooms

½ red pepper

½ green pepper

salt and freshly ground pepper

200g/7oz Mozzarella cheese

1. Cut the dough into quarters. Roll out and use to line 4 greased flan tins.

2. Spread the tomato purée evenly over the dough and sprinkle with oregano and Parmesan cheese.
3. Skin and slice the tomatoes. Place on the pastry bases.

4. Pile on top the shrimps and mussels. Cut the ham into strips and slice the salami. Distribute over the pizzas.
5. Slice the button mushrooms and cut the cleaned peppers into strips. Scatter over the top. Sprinkle with salt and pepper.
6. Slice the Mozzarella cheese and add.
7. Bake in a preheated oven 200°C, 400°F, Gas Mark 6 for 15 to 20 minutes. Serve immediately.

Pizza Bolognese

(Pizza with Bolognese Sauce)

Serves 4:

4 tbsp olive oil

400g/14oz mixed minced meats

1 onion

3 garlic cloves

1 tsp salt

1 tsp cayenne pepper

1 tsp curry powder

1 tbsp oregano

1 small can peeled tomatoes

2 tbsp tomato purée

1 pimiento

salt

freshly ground pepper

pinch mixed spices

8 tomatoes

1 recipe shortcrust pastry (page 28)

50g/2oz breadcrumbs

250g/8oz Emmenthal cheese, grated

chopped parsley, to garnish

1. Heat the oil in a pan and quickly brown the mince.
2. Finely chop the onion. Crush the garlic in salt. Add to the pan and fry until softened.
3. Season with the cayenne pepper, curry powder and oregano. Add the peeled tomatoes.
4. Stir in the tomato purée. Finely dice the pepper. Add to the mince with salt, pepper and mixed spices.
5. Cook over a high heat until all the liquid has evaporated.
6. Meanwhile, skin the tomatoes and slice.
7. Cut the dough into quarters. Roll out and use to line 4 greased pizza or flan tins.
8. Sprinkle the breadcrumbs over the dough. Arrange the slices of tomato over the dough.
9. Spread the mince mixture over the tomatoes, then sprinkle with the cheese.
10. Bake in a preheated oven at 200°C, 400°F, Gas Mark 6 for 15 to 20 minutes. Serve sprinkled with parsley.

NOTES

Pizzas with a bread dough base are becoming increasingly popular. This recipe contains yeast as a raising agent. But even tastier is the genuine sour dough. It is possible to make this type of dough at home, but simpler to buy it from the baker. Try using dough made from strong flour for your bread pizzas.

Bread Dough

Serves 4:

500g/1lb strong flour
1 small sachet of dried yeast
1 tbsp salt
1 tbsp sugar
1 tsp ground caraway seeds
15g/½oz lard
300 ml/½ pint warm water

1. Sift the flour into a bowl.

2. Add the yeast, salt, sugar and caraway seeds.

3. Rub and grate in the lard.

4. Add the warm water and knead until you have a firm dough.

5. Cover, then set aside for about 30 minutes in a warm place.

6. Knead the dough once more and roll out on a floured work surface.

Focaccia

(Bread Pizza)

Serves 4:

1 recipe bread dough (page 34)

100g/4oz ham

50g/2oz stuffed olives

50g/2oz black olives

4 garlic cloves

olive oil

2 egg yolks, beaten

1 tbsp caraway seeds

2 tbsp coarse salt

1 tbsp coriander seeds

1. Cut the bread dough into quarters. Roll out on a floured work surface and use to line 4 greased pizza or flan tins.

2. Cut the ham into strips and place on the dough with the olives.

3. Chop the garlic and sprinkle between the ham and olives.

4. Brush with oil. Bake in a preheated oven at 200°C, 400°F, Gas Mark 6 for about 20 minutes.

5. About 5 minutes before the end of the cooking time, brush the pastry with the egg yolk, then sprinkle with the caraway seeds, salt and coriander. Serve hot or cold.

Focaccia agli Odori e Pomodoro

(Bread Pizza with Herbs and Tomatoes)

Serves 4:

1 recipe bread dough (page 34)

4 garlic cloves

8 tomatoes

sprig basil, chopped

sprig oregano, chopped

salt and freshly ground pepper

pinch mixed spices

100g/4oz Parmesan cheese, grated

1. Cut the bread dough into quarters. Roll out on a floured work surface and use to line 4 greased pizza or flan tins.
2. Chop the garlic and press into the dough.
3. Skin and slice the tomatoes, then place on the dough.
4. Sprinkle the herbs over the tomatoes.
5. Season with salt, pepper and mixed spices.
6. Sprinkle with the cheese. Bake in a preheated oven at 200°C, 400°F, Gas Mark 6 for about 20 minutes. Serve hot or cold.

Pizza Acciughe

(Anchovy Pizza)

Serves 4:

1 recipe bread dough (page 34)

4 tbsp tomato purée

8 tomatoes

2 onions

8 slices ham

4 garlic cloves

100g/4oz anchovy fillets

100g/4oz black olives

1 tbsp oregano

salt

freshly ground pepper

100g/4oz Provolone cheese, grated

1. Cut the bread dough into quarters. Roll out on a floured work surface and use to line 4 greased pizza or flan tins.
2. Spread the dough evenly with tomato purée.
3. Skin and slice the tomatoes. Chop the onions. Cut the ham into strips. Scatter the tomatoes, onions and ham over the dough.
4. Chop the garlic and sprinkle over the mixture.
5. Garnish with anchovy strips in a lattice pattern. Place the olives in the lattice.
6. Season with oregano, salt and pepper. Sprinkle with the cheese.
7. Bake in a preheated oven at 200°C, 400°F, Gas Mark 6 for about 20 minutes. Serve immediately.

Pizza alla Boscaiola

(Woodcutter's Pizza)

Serves 4:

100g/4oz streaky bacon, cubed

25g/1oz butter or margarine

2 garlic cloves

1 tsp salt

1 onion

1 small can peeled tomatoes

1 tsp oregano

freshly ground pepper

pinch mixed spices

For the filling:

100g/4oz button mushrooms

1 small red pepper

1 small green pepper

100g/4oz pepper salami

1 can tuna fish

4 chillies

stuffed olives

Also:

1 recipe bread dough (page 34)

200g/7oz Bel Paese cheese, grated

chopped chives, to garnish

1. Heat the butter in a pan and lightly fry the bacon.
2. Finely chop the garlic in the salt. Finely chop the onion. Fry quickly.
3. Drain the tomatoes and cook until the moisture has evaporated.
4. Season with oregano, salt, pepper and mixed spices. Allow to cool.
5. Meanwhile, slice the mushrooms. Cut the peppers into strips.
6. Cut the salami into strips. Drain and flake the tuna.
7. Cut the bread dough into quarters. Roll out on a floured work surface and use to line 4 greased pizza or flan tins.
8. Cover the dough with the tomato mixture and filling.
9. Bake in a preheated oven at 200°C, 400°F, Gas Mark 6 for 20 minutes.
10. About 5 minutes before the end of cooking, sprinkle with cheese. Serve sprinkled with chives.

Calzone con Carne e Gorgonzola

(Meat and Gorgonzola Calzone)

Serves 4:

200g/7oz cooked veal

1 onion

4 tomatoes

100g/4oz grapes

100g/4oz radicchio

1 tsp thyme

1 tsp oregano

salt

freshly ground pepper

1 bunch chives

150g/5oz blue cheese

1 recipe bread dough (page 34)

1. Cut the veal into cubes. Chop the onion into small pieces.
2. Skin and seed the tomatoes, and dice.
3. Halve and stone the grapes. Cut the radicchio into strips.
4. Put all the ingredients in a bowl and mix carefully. Season with thyme, oregano, salt and pepper.
5. Finely chop the chives. Crumble the blue cheese. Stir into the veal mixture.
6. Cut the bread dough into quarters. Roll out on a floured work surface.

7. Distribute the filling on one half of each piece of dough. Fold over into a pasty shape, pressing the edges together.
8. Place on a greased baking tray. Bake in a preheated oven at 200°C, 400°F, Gas Mark 6 for about 20 minutes. Serve immediately.

Pizza Spinaci alla Contadina

(Peasant Spinach Pizza)

Serves 4:

100g/4oz streaky bacon

25g/1oz butter or margarine

200g/7oz frozen spinach, thawed

salt

freshly ground pepper

pinch grated nutmeg

pinch mixed spices

1 recipe bread dough (page 34)

100g/4oz salami

4 tomatoes

1 tbsp basil

4 eggs, hard boiled

200g/7oz Mozzarella cheese

chopped parsley, to garnish

1. Dice the bacon. Heat the butter in a pan and lightly fry the bacon.
2. Add the well-drained spinach and warm through.
3. Season with salt, pepper, nutmeg and mixed spices, then allow to cool.
4. Meanwhile, cut the bread dough into quarters. Roll out on a floured work surface and use to line 4 greased pizza or flan tins.

6. Season with basil, salt and pepper. Slice the hard-boiled eggs and decorate.
7. Slice the Mozzarella and top the pizza. Bake in a preheated oven at 200°C, 400°F, Gas Mark 6 for 20 minutes. Serve sprinkled with parsley.

5. Cover evenly with the spinach. Peel and slice the tomatoes. Arrange over the spinach. Slice the salami and add.

Pasta

When you mention pasta in Italy, you must also include sauce. *Sugo* and the many varieties of *salsa* are specialities of Italian cuisine. Each region, each town and each family have their individual recipe.

Stories about the origin of pasta abound. Most likely it can be attributed to the Sicilians. In any case, it was from 18th-century Sicily that it made its triumphant progress through Italy and the whole world.

Today, delicious pasta dishes provide quick, filling meals at economical cost.

NOTES

Mass-produced pasta is made from fine flour obtained from the heart of the durum (hard) wheat grain. In the home, strong flour is usually used.

Pasta will keep almost indefinitely. The finished pasta must be allowed to dry carefully, then it can be stored in screw-top jars.

Pasta Dough

Serves 4:

400g/14oz strong flour

4 eggs

1 tsp salt

1-2 tbsp olive oil

1. Sift the flour on to a work surface and make a well in the centre.

2. Add the eggs, salt and oil.

3. With your hands, knead into an elastic consistency.

4. Wrap the pasta dough in a damp cloth. Leave in the refrigerator for 15 minutes.

5. Roll out the dough until almost transparent.

6. Cut out the dough into the required pasta shapes.

Spaghetti della Massaia

(Cook's Recipe)

Serves 4:

4 tbsp olive oil

250g/8oz mixed minced meats

2 garlic cloves

1 tsp salt

4 spring onions

1 carrot

1 tbsp tomato purée

250ml/8 fl oz red wine

250ml/8 fl oz meat stock

1 can peeled tomatoes

1 tbsp basil

1 tsp oregano

salt

freshly ground pepper

pinch mixed spices

400g/14oz spaghetti

chopped chives, to garnish

100g/4oz Pecorino cheese, grated

1. Heat the oil in a pan and brown the meat.
2. Crush the garlic in the salt and fry with the meat.
3. Dice the spring onions and carrot. Add to the meat.

4. Stir in the tomato purée. Pour in the red wine, meat stock and tomatoes. Cover and simmer for 40 minutes.

5. Season with the basil, oregano, salt, pepper and mixed spices.
6. Cook the pasta in boiling salted water for 10 to 15 minutes until *al dente* (that is, firm to the bite).
7. Drain the pasta. Serve topped with the sauce and sprinkled with chopped chives and cheese.

Conchiglie con Cozze

(Conchiglie with Mussels)

Serves 4:

1.5kg/3lb fresh mussels, in shells

1 onion

1 bunch spring onions

1 carrot

50g/2oz butter or margarine

4 garlic cloves

1 tsp salt

250ml/8 fl oz white wine

475ml/16 fl oz meat stock

2 bay leaves

1 can peeled tomatoes

salt

freshly ground pepper

pinch sugar

sprig oregano

sprig parsley

juice from 1 lemon

400g/14oz conchiglie

1. Scrub and pick over the mussels.
2. Cut the onion, spring onions and carrot into strips. Heat the butter in a

large pan and gently fry the vegetables until softened.
3. Crush the garlic in the salt. Add to the pan with the white wine, meat stock, bay leaves and tomatoes. Bring to the boil.
4. Season with salt, pepper and sugar.
5. Add the mussels to the mixture and cook until the mussels have opened. (Discard any that remain closed.)
6. Meanwhile, chop the herbs. Add just before the end of the cooking time and sprinkle with lemon juice.
7. Boil the pasta in salted water for 10 to 15 minutes. Drain well.
8. Dish up on plates and serve with the mussels.

Spaghetti Matriciana

(Spaghetti with Tomatoes and Ham)

Serves 4:

2 garlic cloves

1 tsp salt

50g/2oz butter or margarine

200g/7oz ham

2 onions

8 medium tomatoes

2 tbsp tomato purée

125ml/4 fl oz white wine

125ml/4 fl oz meat stock

salt

freshly ground pepper

pinch sugar

pinch mixed spices

sprig basil

400g/14oz spaghetti

100g/4oz Parmesan cheese, grated

1. Crush the garlic in the salt. Heat the butter in a pan and gently fry the garlic.

2. Cut the ham into thin strips. Dice the onions. Fry until soft but not browned.
3. Skin and chop the tomatoes and add to the ham mixture.

4. Stir in the tomato purée, then add the white wine and stock.
5. Season with salt, pepper, sugar and mixed spices.
6. Finely chop the basil. Mix into the sauce.
7. Boil the spaghetti in salted water for 10 to 15 minutes until *al dente*.
8. Drain the pasta and cover with sauce. Sprinkle with the grated cheese.

Farfalle con Frutti di Mare

(Farfalle with Seafood)

Serves 4:

1 onion
½ red pepper
½ green pepper
1 carrot
50g/2oz butter or margarine
150g/5oz prawns or shrimps
150g/5oz prepared squid
150g/5oz canned tuna fish in oil
150g/5oz shelled mussels
100g/4oz black olives
1 can peeled tomatoes
125ml/4 fl oz red vermouth
250ml/8 fl oz meat stock
salt
freshly ground pepper
pinch mixed spices
400g/14oz farfalle
chopped peppermint, to garnish
chopped chives, to garnish

1. Dice the onion, peppers and carrot. Heat the butter in a pan and gently fry the vegetables.
2. Rinse the prawns or shrimps. Dice the squid. Flake the tuna fish. Add to the pan with the mussels and olives, and allow to cook for 5 minutes.

3. Stir in the tomatoes, vermouth and stock.
4. Season with salt, pepper and mixed spices.
5. Boil the pasta in salted water for 10 to 15 minutes. Remove and drain.
6. Serve the pasta, covered with the sauce and sprinkled with the chopped herbs.

Maccheroni alla Toscana

(Tuscan-style Macaroni)

Serves 4:

400g/14oz cooked veal

4 tbsp olive oil

1 onion

200g/7oz button mushrooms

2 tbsp flour

250ml/8 fl oz meat stock

125ml/4 fl oz white wine

150ml/¼ pint crème fraîche

salt

freshly ground pepper

Worcestershire sauce

75g/3oz blue cheese

400g/14oz macaroni

100g/4oz Pecorino cheese, grated

chopped chives, to garnish

1. Dice the veal. Heat the oil in a large pan and fry the meat. Remove and keep warm.
2. Chop the onion and fry in the remaining oil until softened.

3. Wipe and slice the mushrooms. Add to the onion and fry gently.

4. Sprinkle in the flour. Pour in the stock and white wine. Simmer until thickened. Fold in the *crème fraîche*.

5. Season with salt, pepper and a few drops of

Worcestershire sauce.
6. Crumble the blue cheese and stir into the sauce with the meat.
7. Boil the macaroni in salted water for 10 to 15 minutes. Remove from the heat and drain.
8. Dish up on plates and cover with the sauce. Sprinkle with the Pecorino and chopped chives.

NOTES

If you want to make coloured pasta at home you have to make sure that the vegetable purées used are fairly dry. You might have to add more flour to the dough. Apart from spinach, the following purées may be used: tomato, carrot, onion and leek. Other colours and flavours can be obtained from tomato purée, saffron and, of course, fresh herbs.

Coloured Pasta Dough

Serves 4:

400g/14oz strong flour

75g/3oz fresh blanched or frozen spinach, thawed

2 eggs

1 tsp salt

pinch grated nutmeg

1 tbsp olive oil

1. Sift the flour on to a work surface and make a well in the centre.

2. Finely chop the spinach and squeeze out in a cloth.

3. Put the spinach, eggs, salt, nutmeg and oil in the centre of the flour.

4. Knead from the outside inwards to form elastic dough.

5. Wrap in a damp cloth and leave in the refrigerator for 30 minutes.

6. Roll out very thinly or put through a pasta machine. Cut into the required pasta shapes.

Tagliatelle alle Consalsa di cozza

(Tagliatelle with Mussel Sauce)

Serves 4:

1 bunch spring onions

½ green pepper

½ red pepper

25g/1oz butter or margarine

4 tomatoes

500g/1lb mussels, shelled

250ml/8 fl oz white wine

150ml/¼ pint crème fraîche

salt

freshly ground pepper

pinch saffron

pinch mixed spices

4 egg yolks

4 tbsp cream

sprig lemon balm

400g/14oz tagliatelle

1. Cut the spring onions and peppers into strips. Heat the butter in a pan and gently fry the vegetables.
2. Skin, seed and dice the tomatoes. Add with the mussels to the vegetables.
3. Pour in the white wine and *crème fraîche*. Simmer until the sauce has thickened.
4. Season with salt, pepper, saffron and mixed spices.
5. Mix the egg yolks with the cream. Remove the mussel sauce from the heat and stir in the egg mixture. Heat until thick but do not boil.
6. Chop the lemon balm and add to the sauce.
7. Boil the pasta for 10 to 15 minutes in salted water and drain well.
8. Dish up on plates, cover with the sauce and serve.

Spaghetti Rosse con Calamari

(Pink Spaghetti with Squid Sauce)

Serves 4:

4 garlic cloves

1 tsp salt

4 tbsp olive oil

1 onion

1 each: carrot, celery stick, leek, parsley root

200g/7oz prepared squid

250ml/8 fl oz red wine

250ml/8 fl oz thickened gravy

2 tbsp tomato purée

4 tomatoes

salt

freshly ground pepper

1 tsp thyme

1 tsp oregano

400g/14oz tomato spaghetti

1. Crush the garlic in the salt. Heat the oil in a pan and gently fry the garlic.

2. Prepare and dice the onion and vegetables. Add to the pan and fry until softened.

3. Dice the squid, add to the vegetables and allow to sweat briefly.
4. Stir the red wine and gravy into the tomato purée, then pour into the pan. Cover and cook over a low heat for 40 to 45 minutes.
5. Skin, seed and dice the tomatoes. Add to the sauce and season with salt, pepper, thyme and oregano.
6. Boil the spaghetti in salted water for 10 to 15 minutes. Remove from the heat and drain well.
7. Dish up on plates, cover with the sauce and serve immediately.

Spaghetti Gialle con Lumache

(Carrot Spaghetti with Snail Sauce)

Serves 4:

| 4 garlic cloves |
| 1 tsp salt |
| 4 tbsp olive oil |
| 1 onion |
| 1 bunch spring onions |
| 1 each: carrot, celery stick, leek, parsley root |
| 1 small can of snails |
| 3 tbsp flour |
| 250ml/8 fl oz Asti spumante |
| 250ml/8 fl oz crème fraîche |
| salt |
| freshly ground pepper |
| 2 tbsp lemon juice |
| pinch mixed spices |
| sprig peppermint |
| 400g/14oz carrot spaghetti |

1. Crush the garlic in the salt. Heat the oil in a pan and fry the garlic for a few minutes.
2. Prepare and dice the vegetables, add to the garlic and allow to sweat.
3. Add the drained snails and sprinkle over the flour.
4. Pour over the Asti spumante and simmer the sauce until thickened.
5. Fold in the *crème fraîche*. Season with salt, pepper, lemon juice and mixed spices.
6. Chop the peppermint and stir into the sauce.
7. Boil the spaghetti in salted water for 10 to 15 minutes. Drain well.
8. Dish up on plates, cover with the sauce and serve.

Pasta con Pane

(Peppermint Noodles with Cream Sauce)

Serves 4:

1 onion

4 tbsp olive oil

250g/8oz ham

1 small can of peas

1 small can of diced carrots

250ml/8 fl oz crème fraîche

150ml/¼ pint cream

50g/2oz Parmesan cheese, grated

salt

freshly ground pepper

pinch grated nutmeg

pinch mixed spices

400g/14oz peppermint noodles

1 bunch chives

1. Finely chop the onion. Heat the oil in a pan and fry the onion until softened.
2. Cut the ham into strips, add to the pan and allow to sweat.
3. Drain the peas and carrots and add to the ham.
4. Add the *crème fraîche*, cream and cheese. Simmer gently until the sauce thickens.
5. Season with salt, pepper, nutmeg and mixed spices.
6. Boil the noodles in salted water for 10 to 15 minutes. Drain well.
7. Dish up on plates and cover with the sauce. Serve sprinkled with chives.

Spaghetti Verdé con Peperonata

(Herb Spaghetti with Peppers)

Serves 4:

300g/10oz fillet steak

100g/4oz streaky bacon

4 tbsp olive oil

1 onion

1 pimiento

1 green pepper

1 red pepper

1 can peeled tomatoes

100g/4oz black and green olives

250ml/8 fl oz thickened gravy

½ tsp cayenne pepper

½ tsp curry powder

salt

freshly ground pepper

1 bunch chives

400g/14oz herb spaghetti

1. Dice the steak and bacon. Heat the oil in a large pan and brown the steak. Remove and keep warm.
2. Fry the bacon in the remaining oil.
3. Finely chop the onion and pimiento. Add to the pan and allow to soften.
4. Cut the peppers into strips. Add to the pan and cook until softened.
5. Stir in the tomatoes, olives and gravy. Simmer until the sauce thickens.
6. Season with cayenne pepper, curry powder, salt and pepper. Finely chop the chives and add. Return the meat to the pan. Heat gently.

7. Cook the pasta in boiling salted water for 10 to 15 minutes. Remove from the heat and drain well.
8. Dish up on plates, cover with the sauce and serve immediately.

NOTES

Lasagne and cannelloni are not alone in being world-famous types of pasta. Nowadays, ravioli, agnolotti and tortellini are just as well known. These small pouches of dough are served in every region with different sorts of filling.

Lasagne

Serves 4:

1 recipe pasta dough (p 48)

For the filling:
4 tbsp olive oil
1 onion
2 garlic cloves
1 tsp salt
250g/8oz minced meat
3 tbsp flour
1 can peeled tomatoes
salt
freshly ground pepper
pinch mixed spices
1 tsp oregano
1 tsp basil
250ml/8 fl oz béchamel sauce (page 55)
200g/7oz Mozzarella cheese
4 tbsp Parmesan cheese, grated

1. Roll out the pasta dough very thinly. Cut into large squares. Allow to dry out for 30 minutes. Cook in boiling salted water for 5 minutes.

2. Finely chop the onion. Crush the garlic in the salt. Heat the oil in a pan and brown the minced meat with the onion and garlic.

3. Sprinkle the mixture with the flour. Add the tomatoes and season with salt, pepper, mixed spices and herbs.

4. Layer the squares of dough, meat and béchamel sauce in a greased soufflé dish. Slice the Mozzarella. Cover the lasagne with both cheeses.

Cannelloni

Serves 4:

1 recipe pasta dough (p 48)

For the filling:
2 garlic cloves
1 tsp salt
4 tbsp olive oil
250g/8oz minced beef
1 onion
salt
freshly ground pepper
1 tsp oregano
1 tsp basil
4 tbsp Parmesan cheese
200g/7oz cheese, grated

1. Roll out the pasta dough very thinly. Cut into large squares. Allow to dry out for 30 minutes. Cook in boiling salted water for 5 minutes.

2. Crush the garlic in the salt. Heat the oil in a pan and brown the meat together with the garlic.

3. Finely chop the onion and add to the pan to soften. Season with salt, pepper, oregano, basil and the Parmesan cheese.

4. Distribute the filling on the squares of dough. Roll them into tubes and layer in a greased soufflé dish. Sprinkle with the cheese and bake.

Lasagne al Forno

(Baked Lasagne)

Serves 4:

4 tbsp olive oil

250g/8oz minced beef

1 onion

2 garlic cloves

1 tsp salt

2 tbsp tomato purée

2 tbsp flour

125ml/4 fl oz red wine

1 can peeled tomatoes

sprig oregano

1 bay leaf, crushed

salt

freshly ground pepper

For the béchamel sauce:

50g/2oz butter or margarine

50g/2oz flour

475ml/16 fl oz milk

pinch grated nutmeg

4 tbsp Parmesan cheese, grated

Also:

400g/14oz pasta dough (page 42)
  or bought lasagne slices

200g/7oz Mozzarella cheese

chopped chives, to garnish

1. Heat the oil in a pan and brown the meat.
2. Finely chop the onion and crush the garlic in the salt. Add to the pan and fry until softened.
3. Stir in the tomato purée and sprinkle with the flour. Add the red wine and tomatoes, and cook until the mixture is a creamy sauce.
4. Finely chop the oregano and add with the bay leaf, salt and pepper.
5. For the béchamel sauce, heat the butter in a pan and stir in the flour.
6. Slowly stir in the milk. Cook, stirring all the time, until the sauce thickens. Season with salt and pepper. Add the nutmeg and cheese.
7. Cook the lasagne slices in boiling salted water for 5 minutes. Take out and set aside.
8. Layer the meat sauce, béchamel sauce and the slices of pasta in a greased soufflé dish.
9. Slice the Mozzarella and cover the lasagne. Place in a preheated oven at 200°C, 400°F, Gas Mark 6 for 15 minutes. Sprinkle with chives and serve.

Lasagne Verde con Verdure

(Green Lasagne with Vegetables)

Serves 4:

1 onion

1 courgette

4 tomatoes

100g/4oz button mushrooms

1 small can peas

For the tomato sauce:

100g/4oz streaky bacon

2 tbsp olive oil

200g/7oz ham

2 tbsp tomato purée

3 tbsp flour

125ml/4 fl oz white wine

1 can peeled tomatoes

1 tsp garlic salt

½ tsp black pepper

pinch mixed spices

sprig basil, chopped

Also:

250ml/8 fl oz béchamel sauce
   (page 55)

400g/14oz green pasta dough
(page 48) or bought lasagne slices

200g/7oz Bel Paese cheese, grated

1. Slice the onion and the courgette.
2. Skin the tomatoes and chop into cubes.
3. Wipe and slice the button mushrooms.
4. Strain the can of peas.
5. For the sauce, dice the bacon. Heat the oil in a pan and brown the bacon.
6. Cut the ham into strips and add to the bacon. Stir in the tomato purée. Sprinkle over the flour, pour in the white wine and add the canned tomatoes.

7. Season with the garlic salt, pepper and mixed spices. Add the chopped basil.
8. Make the béchamel sauce and set aside. Cook the pasta in boiling salted water for 5 minutes and drain.
9. Layer the tomato sauce, slices of pasta, the prepared vegetables and béchamel sauce in a greased soufflé dish.
10. Sprinkle evenly with the cheese. Bake in a preheated oven at 200°C, 400°F, Gas Mark 6 for about 15 minutes. Serve immediately.

Cannelloni con Fegato D'Oca

(Cannelloni with Liver)

Serves 4:

250g/8oz chicken livers

4 tbsp olive oil

1 onion

1 carrot

2 tomatoes

1 tsp thyme

1 tsp marjoram

2 tbsp tomato purée

3 tbsp flour

juice of 1 lemon

125ml/4 fl oz white wine

salt

freshly ground pepper

pinch mixed spices

3 tbsp butter or margarine

400g/14oz pasta dough (page 42)
   or bought cannelloni

250ml/8 fl oz béchamel sauce
   (page 55)

50g/2oz Pecorino cheese

200g/7oz Bel Paese cheese, grated

chopped parsley, to garnish

1. Rinse and drain the liver, and chop into small pieces. Heat the oil in a frying pan and fry the liver. Remove and keep warm.
2. Dice the onion and carrot. Add to the remaining fat and cook until softened.
3. Skin and chop the tomatoes. Add to the pan. Season with the thyme and marjoram.

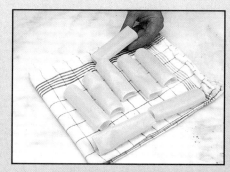

4. Stir in the tomato purée. Blend the flour with the lemon juice and white wine. Pour into the pan to thicken the vegetables.
5. Add the liver. Season with salt and pepper, and allow to cool.
6. Grease an ovenproof dish with the butter.
7. Cook the cannelloni in boiling salted water for about 5 minutes. Stuff with the liver mixture.
8. Layer in the dish. Season the béchamel sauce with the Pecorino cheese and pour over the cannelloni. Sprinkle with the Bel Paese cheese.
9. Bake in a preheated oven at 200°C, 400°F, Gas Mark 6 for about 15 minutes. Serve sprinkled with chopped parsley.

Cannelloni con Gamberetti

(Cannelloni with Prawns)

Serves 4:

1 bunch spring onions

2 tbsp butter or margarine

400g/14oz prawns

4 tomatoes

100g/4oz button mushrooms

125ml/4 fl oz white wine

2 tbsp flour

salt

freshly ground pepper

pinch mixed spices

sprig lemon balm

400g/14oz pasta dough (page 42)
    or bought cannelloni

4 tbsp butter or margarine

250ml/8 fl oz thickened tomato
sauce (page 56)

200g/7oz Mozzarella cheese

1. Finely slice the spring onions. Heat the butter in a pan and cook the spring onions until softened.
2. Rinse the prawns. Skin, seed and dice the tomatoes. Add both to the onions.
3. Wipe clean the button mushrooms, slice and add to the pan.
4. Blend the wine with the flour. Pour into the pan to thicken the vegetable mixture.
5. Season with salt, pepper and mixed spices. Chop the lemon balm and add. Allow the mixture to cool.
6. Cook the cannelloni in boiling salted water for about 5 minutes. Drain well and stuff with the prawn and vegetable mixture.
7. Grease an ovenproof dish with the butter. Layer the cannelloni in the dish.
8. Pour over the tomato sauce. Slice the Mozzarella cheese and cover the cannelloni.
9. Bake in a preheated oven at 200°C, 400°F, Gas Mark 6 for about 15 minutes.

Ravioli agli Spinaci

(Ravioli with Spinach)

Serves 4:

400g/14oz pasta dough (page 42)

For the filling:
100g/4oz frozen spinach, thawed

100g/4oz sausagemeat

1 egg

1 tbsp mustard

salt

freshly ground pepper

pinch grated nutmeg

1 tbsp basil

1-2 tbsp breadcrumbs

For the sauce:
50g/2oz butter or margarine

100g/4oz streaky bacon

1 onion

4 tomatoes

1 small can peeled tomatoes

sprig basil, chopped

pinch mixed spices

1. Roll out the dough very thinly on a floured work surface. Cut into small squares. Allow the dough to dry out for 10 minutes.
2. Meanwhile, finely chop the spinach. In a bowl, mix together the spinach, sausagemeat, egg and mustard.
3. Season with salt, pepper, nutmeg and basil. If necessary, bind with breadcrumbs.

4. Distribute the spinach mixture on half the squares. Brush the edges with water.

5. Place the remaining squares on top and press the edges together.
6. Cook the ravioli in boiling salted water for 5 to 10 minutes, according to size.
7. For the sauce, dice the bacon. Heat the butter in a pan and brown the bacon.
8. Finely chop the onion. Cook until softened.
9. Skin, seed and chop the tomatoes. Add to the mixture.
10. Sieve the peeled tomatoes and top up the mixture. Simmer until thick.
11. Season with basil, salt, pepper and mixed spices.
12. Drain the ravioli, cover with tomato sauce and serve immediately.

Agnolotti con Luccio

(Agnolotti with Pike)

Serves 4:

400g/14oz pasta dough (page 42)

For the filling:
250g/8oz pike fillets

1 egg

2 tbsp flour

2 tbsp stock

sprig parsley, chopped

sprig dill, chopped

2 tbsp lemon juice

Worcestershire sauce

salt

freshly ground pepper

pinch grated nutmeg

For the sauce:
50g/2oz butter or margarine

50g/2oz flour

250ml/8 fl oz meat stock

250ml/8 fl oz white wine

150ml/¼ pint cream

100g/4oz Parmesan cheese, grated

pinch mixed spices

1. Roll out the dough on a floured work surface. Shape into small stars. Allow the dough to dry out for 10 minutes.

2. Meanwhile, mince the pike fillets and place in a bowl.

3. Add the egg, flour, stock and chopped parsley and dill. Mix to a firm consistency.

4. Season with the lemon juice, a few drops of Worcestershire sauce, salt, pepper and nutmeg. Distribute the mixture over half the star shapes. Brush the edges with water.

5. Place the remaining half of stars on top and press the edges together.

6. Cook the agnolotti in boiling salted water for 5 to 10 minutes, according to size.

7. For the sauce, heat the butter in a pan and stir in the flour.

8. Top up with meat stock, white wine and cream. Simmer until thick.

9. Fold in the cheese. Season with salt, pepper and mixed spices.

10. Drain the agnolotti and dish up on plates. Cover with sauce and serve immediately.

Soups

· The Italians are adventurous
when making soups, and often
use many different fresh
vegetables combined with
meat, poultry and fish. A little
pasta added to soup makes it
more nutritious, interesting
and transforms soup into an
ideal light meal on its own.
Use small pasta shapes, such
as miniature shells, small
rings, ditalini, small wheels,
soup noodles or pasta
alphabets.

If you are freezing soup,
add the pasta when reheating.

Minestra di Trippa

(Tripe Soup)

Serves 4:

500g/1lb calf's tripe

4 tbsp olive oil

100g/4oz streaky bacon

1 onion

100g/4oz celeriac

2 carrots

1 leek

250ml/8 fl oz white wine

1 litre/1¾ pints meat stock

2-4 cloves

1 bay leaf

50g/2oz small pasta shapes

salt

freshly ground pepper

3 tbsp cider vinegar

juice of ½ lemon

pinch of sugar

chopped chives, to garnish

chopped dill, to garnish

1. Wash the tripe. Cut into strips and blanch in salted water for 5 minutes. Remove and rinse again.
2. Cut the bacon into cubes. Heat the oil in a pan and gently fry the bacon.
3. Add the tripe and fry.
4. Dice the onion, celeriac, carrots and leek. Add the vegetables to the tripe and leave to soften.
5. Top up with the white wine and stock. Season with the cloves and bay leaf. Cover and simmer for about 50 minutes, adding the pasta after 45 minutes.
6. Season with salt, pepper, vinegar, lemon juice and sugar. Serve garnished with chopped chives and dill.

Minestra di Verdure

(Vegetable and Noodle Soup)

Serves 4:

2 chicken breasts

3 tbsp olive oil

2 garlic cloves

1 tsp salt

1 bunch spring onions

2 carrots

100g/4oz celery

1 red pepper

1 tbsp tomato purée

250ml/8 fl oz white wine

1 litre/1¾ pints meat stock

1 bay leaf

1 tsp thyme

1 tsp rosemary

100g/4oz soup noodles

salt

freshly ground pepper

chopped parsley, to garnish

100g/4oz Parmesan cheese, grated

1. Dice the chicken breasts. Heat the oil in a pan and brown the chicken.
2. Crush the garlic in the salt and fry.
3. Cut the vegetables into thin strips. Add to the meat.
4. Stir in the tomato purée. Pour in the white wine and top up with the stock.
5. Season with the bay leaf, thyme and rosemary. Simmer for 10 minutes.
6. Add the noodles and cook for 5 to 8 minutes, according to size.
7. Season with salt and pepper. Serve garnished with chopped parsley and grated cheese.

Zuppa di Pesce alla Genovese

(Genoese Fish Soup)

Serves 4:

2 garlic cloves

1 tsp salt

4 tbsp olive oil

1 onion

1 bunch spring onions

1 red pepper

100g/4oz prepared squid

100g/4oz mussels, shelled

100g/4oz prawns

1 small can peeled tomatoes

250ml/8 fl oz white wine

¾ litre/1¼ pints meat stock

1 bay leaf

2 cloves

100g/4oz miniature pasta shells or soup noodles

salt

freshly ground pepper

1 tbsp basil

chopped chives and parsley, to garnish

1. Chop the garlic in the salt. Heat the oil in a pan and gently fry the garlic.
2. Cut the vegetables into strips. Add to the pan to soften.
3. Add the squid, mussels and prawns. Top up with the tomatoes, white wine and stock. Simmer for 10 minutes.
4. Add the bay leaf, cloves and noodles. Simmer for a further 5 minutes.
5. Season with salt, pepper and basil. Serve garnished with chopped chives and parsley.

Index

W. Foulsham & Company Limited
Yeovil Road, Slough, Berkshire, SL1 4JH

Originally published by Falken Verlag GmbH, West Germany.

This English language edition copyright © 1989 W. Foulsham & Co Ltd

ISBN 0–572–01450–3

Printed in Great Britain

Translated by Agnes Rook